The Secret of a Meeting:

Use Intimate Get-Togethers to Create Meaningful Connections

By

Gerard K. Walker

The Secret of a Meeting: Use Intimate Get-Togethers to Create Meaningful Connections

The Secret of a Meeting: Use Intimate Get-Togethers to Create Meaningful Connections

TABLE OF CONTENTS

The Secret of a Meeting: Use Intimate Get-Togethers to Create Meaningful Connections

Introduction

In the past, I have been a guest at a lavish party held in celebration of the Super Bowl. There were several famous people present, including a former football player who is now retired. Delicious appetizers and refreshing cocktails were provided by a few of San Francisco's most acclaimed chefs and bartenders. The main hall included a lifelike replica of the Golden Gate Bridge as well as real seals swimming in a tank that greeted guests with wet kisses as they entered the major event. The replica of the Golden Gate Bridge stood tall in the main hall. The amount of buzz that surrounded this event led me to believe that it would be the best party I'd ever been to, but the reality was quite different.

Since then, I haven't been able to stop pondering the following question: What are the characteristics of a fantastic party? By reading this book, you will be able to narrow down the solution I came to. Even if the party is enjoyable without these elements, the following morning, when your guests wake up, they won't remark to

The Secret of a Meeting: Use Intimate Get-Togethers to Create Meaningful Connections

themselves, "That party was unbelievable!" Take the Trip of reading this book to ensure that your guests will not be able to stop talking about your wonderful celebration even several weeks after the final bottle of champagne has burst. It has never been so easy to cultivate meaningful ties and build friendships.

LET'S GO!!

Chapter 1: What you should know to start? – The 4Ws

1. Why?

Putting on a party requires a lot of effort. When you take into consideration everything that you need to organize, such as sending out invitations and requesting RSVPs, preparing finger foods and determining how much alcohol to purchase, and compiling a playlist of songs to play during the event, the list of things that need to be done is extensive.

It may come as a relief to learn that all the effort you are putting in is building excellent habits and is wonderful for your health and wellness, even though it may seem like a mission.

This is the reason why.

The Secret of a Meeting: Use Intimate Get-Togethers to Create Meaningful Connections

You will acquire the ability to deal with stress

If party planning isn't your day job, then throwing an occasional get-together can be a difficult endeavor. Some professionals think that being aware of your stress can provide your body with additional energy and prompt you to enter a state of reactivity, which is a positive outcome. You will be better able to handle other difficult situations in your life if you learn how to deal with stress and even learn to embrace it.

Helps you become more organized and efficient

How would you evaluate your ability to manage your time? When it comes to party planning and preparation, it's important to know how to prioritize tasks so that you don't become bogged down in any one of them.

Have you taken on more than you can handle? Think about handing up certain responsibilities or streamlining the plans you've made. When it comes to party planning, making decisions on the food that will be served is one of the tasks that take the most time. Will you be providing finger foods, or would you prefer to do something a little bit fancier and have a sit-down meal? This may be determined, in part, by the number of people you expect to attend as well as the quantity of space available.

If everything becomes too much to handle, you might want to consider outsourcing the catering. Our catering staff in Perth is well-known for providing mouthwatering finger foods, regardless of the size of the audience they are serving.

Time management is a valuable skill that may help you become more productive in many aspects of your life. And it helps the party go off without a hitch.

It will motivate you to clean your house

It's no secret that nobody enjoys cleaning, but when there's a party on the horizon, your place may need a good spray and wipe to get it look like it's ready for the big event. The process of decluttering provides you with an additional incentive to get rid of things that you may not necessarily use or need anymore, so making more space for your group of friends to interact with one another.

You will have the opportunity to sample new finger foods

If you enjoy being inventive in the kitchen, throwing a party is a fantastic opportunity to test out some new recipes. It is even simpler if you schedule catering because you won't have to spend hours laboriously preparing finger foods for everyone. This is especially helpful if the food you intend to offer is time-consuming to prepare from scratch.

Brings about a positive state of mind and positive vibes

After a typical week, everyone will appreciate having something to look forward to, and throwing a party is a fun way to do so. Spending quality time with friends has been shown to reduce stress levels by lowering cortisol levels and increasing the production of feel-good chemicals. Think of it as a pick-me-up for your disposition!

Can help reduce anxiety

Hosting a party can assist you in strengthening your social skills and overcoming any social anxiety you may encounter, which is helpful if you are someone who can feel uncomfortable around other people at times. When you play host, you are obligated to engage in conversation with all of your guests, and when your guests bring friends of their own, you have the chance to cultivate new friendships.

Daytime celebrations are a great way to soak up some vitamin D

If you hold a party during the day outside, your skin will thank you for the vitamin D, which is something that a lot of people, including ourselves, tend to be deficient in. There are also other potential health benefits.

You'll have a more restful night's sleep as a result.

The Secret of a Meeting: Use Intimate Get-Togethers to Create Meaningful Connections

The preparation for a party requires a lot of energy, which is why it results in a restful night's sleep. At the end of the night, you will be so exhausted that you will be able to immediately fall asleep on your pillow without any thoughts running through your head about the things you have to do the following day.

2. When?

The following is a list of general rules:

1. The best night of the week is always Friday.

Friday Night activities are hosted by a very small percentage of people, but even birthday celebrations can be better suited.

2. Compared to Sundays, Saturdays are almost usually busier.

The Secret of a Meeting: Use Intimate Get-Togethers to Create Meaningful Connections

A lot of households may be considering moving their get-togethers to Saturdays rather than Sundays so that they won't conflict with religious services. In contrast, research has shown that Saturdays see five times the number of guests as Sundays do when it comes to celebrations. If you have your party on a Saturday, rather than on a Sunday afternoon, you greatly increase the likelihood of having to compete with other events and activities that are also taking place at the same time.

3. Don't discount the possibility of weekends during national holidays.

Even though several households travel during long weekends, virtually no one hosts gatherings during those times. In particular, if you are hosting a marketing or business event, this is the time of year when your customers do not have any other arrangements already established.

4. Avoid doing it on the weekend that comes AFTER a weekend that falls on a federal holiday.

The weekends that FOLLOW three-day weekends are typically jam-packed with activities such as errands, parties that were postponed, and almost anything else you can think of that was moved back by a week. These two weekends are without fail the busiest of the entire year.

THEN THINK ABOUT THE TIME

The timing of a party is very important, and it will be easier for you to establish when the party should begin and end if you have a better sense of what the party will entail and who will be attending.

It is also important to think about how long the party will go; it is usually great to have a start and finish time in mind so that attendees will be better aware of what is expected of them, and they will be able to make arrangements for transportation or babysitters, and you won't have the problem of having to ask people to leave at the end of the party! You can also make certain that you have adequate time to carry out whatever other activities you have planned for the party, such as eating, entertainment, and so on.

Among the available choices are:

- Stay away from the "peak" hours: The busiest times of the day for people to host parties are from 11 am to 4 pm on Saturdays and from 12 pm to 3 pm on Sundays. You will be in fine shape as long as you can avoid these two peak hours. Either start the day bright and early with brunch or hold off on the meal until the evening to ensure that your guests won't need to set their alarm clocks.

- A party serving cocktails would be perfect for the early evening or late (people should be allowed to eat before or after the event).

- It is recommended that children's parties be approximately two hours long in the morning because this is the time of day when the children are at their most active, they can play before sitting down for food, and you allow parents to still be able to do family activities in the afternoon (it also tends to work better around sleep times for very little children).

- Parties in the style of a family barbecue are most successful in the middle of the afternoon or early evening, preferably around tea time but not too late for younger children.

3. Where?

It's possible that throwing a party will take a lot of work, but in the end, it'll probably be worth it. The location of the event should be one of the first things you think about. The location of the party needs to be somewhere that offers a variety of entertaining activities, has sufficient space for all of the invited attendees, and does not detract from the party's overall atmosphere. No matter where you live, there is a plethora of choices when it comes to locations where you may host a party of any size.

The Secret of a Meeting: Use Intimate Get-Togethers to Create Meaningful Connections

Your Residence

Even though it will be a lot of effort for you as the host or hostess, the least complicated alternative is to have the party at your own home. At your home, you have complete command over everything. You might think about hiring a catering company or waiting for staff if you do not want to spend the entirety of your party worrying about preparing food, cleaning up after it, or serving guests.

A dining establishment or a pub

If you would prefer not to do any work during the party or worry about things getting ruined in your house, a restaurant or bar is a nice place to throw a party depending on the age of the visitors in attendance. Simply calling ahead, explaining your predicament, and reserving a table is all that is required if the number of people in your party can be accommodated at a single table. If you are planning on hosting a larger gathering, it is highly recommended that you make reservations at the restaurant or bar at least one or two months in advance.

The Secret of a Meeting: Use Intimate Get-Togethers to Create Meaningful Connections

You can make a party menu for your guests to choose from by selecting a few things from the usual menu of the restaurant if you will have a large number of people attending your event. If you're celebrating a special occasion and want to bring your cake to the restaurant, some places will let you do so, regardless of how large your gathering is. Simply double-verify before we go.

A Public Park

When the conditions are right, parks provide for fantastic locations for hosting huge gatherings. There is a large amount of open space as well as playgrounds, and typically there are also basketball, baseball, and soccer fields for guests to use. The majority of parks also provide pavilions for hire, which come equipped with picnic tables, grills, and occasionally even kitchens.

Rooftop

Because most people do not have parties or other events in this kind of setting, throwing your party on a rooftop is one method to give it an air of exclusivity and draw more people to attend. In addition, the views that can be enjoyed from a rooftop can be extremely stunning and add an air of atmosphere. During the warmer months, this is a wonderful alternative for hosting gatherings.

In addition, hosting a party on a rooftop can be an excellent way to make the most of a large city by providing guests with a view of the city's skyline as well as the activity that takes place on the ground below.

The only catch is that it might easily be ruined by bad weather, so you should make sure to have a backup plan close by.

It's a boat or a yacht.

Bringing a body of water into the setting of your party can instill a sense of freedom and adventure in the guests. As a result of the limited number of people who have the opportunity to host on a boat or yacht, the event will exude an air of opulence and privilege to those who attend.

The Secret of a Meeting: Use Intimate Get-Togethers to Create Meaningful Connections

The majority of boats and yachts have all of the conveniences that passengers require. Things like a bar, a kitchen, and sound systems are all examples of this.

This option is reserved for the guests of the celebration who have the most life experience. If you do not know someone who owns a boat, it will be tough and expensive, and it will also be difficult to schedule everyone's arrival in time for the boat to leave.

In Other Locations

You can throw a party in an amusement park, a bowling alley, a movie theater, a theme restaurant, or any other kind of activity center if you want to go somewhere that offers a lot of things to do and see. You can start the party at your house, then proceed to your destination, and then leave from there or end the party at your house as well. Many of these locations have designated party rooms that you can use, but you also have the option of ending the party at your house. Call ahead to inquire about any special party packages or discounted rates that may be available, and double-check that the location you've picked is suitable for the guests' ages. If you are going somewhere with a huge number of youngsters, such as a large amusement park, you need also to make sure that there are sufficient adults to monitor everyone's safety.

4. Who?

The fact is that to have an incredible party, you need to invite an incredible crowd. Being careful with the guest list can go a long way, even though it may be seductive to invite the usual suspects or to give it an open invitation. This can make a big difference. The following are some pointers to keep in mind to make sure the guests are having a good time, the atmosphere is lively, and the gathering is a success.

Take part in the game of numbers.

Before you send out invitations, you should determine how many people you will be able to comfortably host based on the size of the venue as well as the amount of money you have budgeted for the food and drinks. Be mindful of the fact that some portion of your invited visitors won't be able to make it to the event. The actual amount will change depending on how far in advance you send the invitations and how well you know the people on your guest list, but a reasonable rule of thumb is to assume that twenty percent of the people you invite will say no. Don't send out too many invitations, but make sure you have enough guests to comfortably fill the area you've set aside for the celebration, whether that's just your dining room table or the entirety of your home. After all, a party that is held in a space that is primarily empty doesn't seem very much like a party at all!

Invite persons who have an existing rapport with one another.

Have you ever attended a party when the only person you knew that was there was the host? Awkward. Even more terrible? After a messy breakup, you walk into the room to find your ex waiting for you there. Make sure that anyone you invite will know at least one other person who will be attending the party unless the guest in issue is someone who is known to be an outgoing extrovert. In addition, you shouldn't count conflict by bringing together individuals who would get along better apart from one another. If you are unsure, you should inquire with the individual who you are more familiar with as to whether or not they would mind if you invited the other person. If you are unable to choose between the two options, you should inform them that they are both invited so that they may choose for themselves whether or not to attend the event.

Change things up on the guest list.

It's fun to bring everyone together for a night of remembering every once in a while, but you might want to think about inviting people from different eras or phases of your life as well. For a party to be enjoyable, there must be room for people to mix and get to know one another, as well as for old friends to get together and catch up with one another. Simply because there is no better way to bring people together than to throw a party.

Include the person who is the center of attention.

Even if everyone in the room gets along, that does not necessarily mean that the atmosphere is positive. You should invite a couple of friends who are charismatic and talkative and who are comfortable chatting with everyone, whether they are also talkative or are more reserved and need an opportunity to open up more.

Chapter 2: How to put things together?

1. Invitations & Reminders

For different types of gatherings, different procedures should be applied.

Intimate Dinner

Guest List: Having the correct combination of people becomes increasingly vital as the size of the gathering decreases. Some people believe that it's a good idea to invite people who already have a lot in common with you, while others believe that it's better to invite people who come from different backgrounds and have different points of view. Spend some time considering what each of your guests can "bring to the table," but ultimately you should trust your gut and go with your first impression.

If you are going to be the one preparing the meal for the evening and will not have any wait staff, make sure that you do not invite more people to eat than you will be able to cook for and serve by yourself. You should also consider the size of your space as well as the amount of money that you are ready to spend. Keep in mind that even if you are the hostess, you may and should take some time to enjoy yourself.

Choosing to Accept an Invitation: Websites such as "Paperless Post" make it simple for hosts of parties to personalize and send out attractive electronic invitations, and it's just as simple for guests to respond. The website "Emilypost.com" offers several helpful suggestions for sending out effective electronic invitations. One of these suggestions is to disable the function that enables recipients to view the names of other people who have been invited, particularly in situations in which the recipients do not know one another. In addition, be sure to approach it as you would a standard invitation and include information about who is hosting the party, the type of party it is, the reason the party is being thrown (if there is a reason), the time and location of the party (with maps, if applicable), and the instructions regarding the RSVP.

The Secret of a Meeting: Use Intimate Get-Togethers to Create Meaningful Connections

When should the invitation be sent: Etiquette experts recommend sending a formal dinner party invitation three to six weeks in advance, while an invitation to an informal soirée should be sent anywhere from a few days to three weeks in advance.

Cocktail Party

Guest List: A cocktail party is suitable for a wide variety of events and celebrations, such as birthdays, anniversaries, holidays, engagement parties, charity events, and so on. Indeed, the kind of beverage you serve will often dictate who you choose to invite, but this isn't always the case. As is the case when planning a wedding, you should begin by selecting what sort of atmosphere you want to create for the evening. This will make it much simpler for you to choose a place. It's possible that you'd want to hold a more relaxed cocktail event at your home. On the other hand, if you're hoping to have a night full of dancing, you'll need a location that supports that.

You'll have a much better sense of how many people you can invite after you have a better grasp on the dimensions

The Secret of a Meeting: Use Intimate Get-Togethers to Create Meaningful Connections

of the venue, as well as whether or not the majority of your guests will be seated for the duration of the event, or whether they will be moving around or dancing instead. Because you want your guests to have a good time, it is essential to take into account the level of comfort they require. As is the case with any party, it is essential to be aware of your budget, as this has a significant bearing on the headcount, particularly if you will need to hire additional hands.

You need to determine if you want to provide low-cost beverages and food to a large number of guests to stay within your budget, or whether you want to serve more gourmet fare to a smaller group of close friends to create a more intimate atmosphere. Even if a cocktail party will have more attendees than an intimate dinner, you should still consider how well your guests will get along with one another (please don't invite any of your guests' enemies!) and, most importantly, if you want them to be a part of your celebration.

The Secret of a Meeting: Use Intimate Get-Togethers to Create Meaningful Connections

Choosing an Invitation: While sending an invitation by email is acceptable, you should be ready to follow up with a phone call if you do not receive an RSVP. In addition, if you are sending out electronic invitations, make use of the medium to send out an alert about the event a couple of days before it is scheduled to take place. You should make every effort to avoid inviting people through a Facebook event because invitees can easily miss it, and Facebook events are only the best option for really big-size gatherings.

When should the invitation be sent: Between one and four weeks in advance, depending on the significance of the event.

Weddings

Guest list:　Determining who to invite to a wedding begins with the future husband and wife reaching an agreement on the maximum amount of money they are willing to spend, as recommended by Martha Stewart, the

The Secret of a Meeting: Use Intimate Get-Togethers to Create Meaningful Connections

authority on all things related to the art of living. Keep in mind that the cost of a buffet is typically lower per person than the cost of a more traditional seated lunch. The next thing that has to be done is for the couple and both of their families to compile a list of close relatives and friends who cannot miss the event under any circumstances. After that, the couple has to select what kind of atmosphere they want to create. For instance, do they foresee a gathering that is smaller and more personal, or one that is larger and more festive, and what sort of location would they ideally desire (garden, ballroom, etc.), in addition to the obvious question of whether or not their budget would allow for it?

When a preliminary list of non-negotiable guests has been created, as well as when the atmosphere and budget have been decided, it is much simpler to determine whether or not coworkers and significant others can be invited to the event. The wives and husbands of the guests are required to be invited, and according to protocol, a pair that is living together, regardless of whether or not they are engaged, is normally treated like a married couple. Regarding the question of whether or not to invite other guests who can bring a plus one, it is always a gesture that is very much appreciated if you have the space and the financial means to do so. After the guest list has been determined, it is time to select those who will get invitations.

Choosing to Accept an Invitation: The type of invitation that is chosen ought to be a representation of the style, tone, and level of formality that will be present at the event, and all of the particulars ought to be simple to comprehend. E-mail invitations are allowed for weddings with a less formal atmosphere (yeah, the times are changing!), but only if all of the attendees have access to email. For example, grandparents may not have access to email. However, keep in mind that many industry professionals believe that wedding invites should never, under any circumstances, be sent by email. The Knot, an online resource for anything and everything linked to weddings suggests utilizing traditional paper because of the added sense of significance it provides.

The Secret of a Meeting: Use Intimate Get-Togethers to
Create Meaningful Connections

When should you send the invitation: According to The Knot, invites should be sent out six to eight weeks in advance to provide guests with sufficient time to clear their schedules and make travel arrangements, if necessary. If the wedding will take place in a faraway location, it is recommended that invitations be sent out three months in advance. It is also a good idea to send out "save the date" cards six to eight months in advance of the wedding date. This will assist ensure that you have a large guest list.

Now go ahead and enjoy yourself!

THERE ARE SOME TIPS FOR THE CHOSEN ONES

When bringing friends around, make sure you exercise discretion and good manners.

Do not distribute invitations or spread the word at your place of employment or school if you will only be inviting a small number of people. It's a good idea to either send your invitations via regular mail or email. You can send invitations covertly, and you are also able to include relevant information in the envelopes, such as your address, driving directions, dress code, or anything else that they may require information about.

Send out your invitations at least a week in advance for a casual get-together, but at least two weeks in advance for a more formal event.

Websites such as Paperless Post make it simple to produce invites that are both personal and adorable. They provide a whole area devoted to invites that may be customized online for no cost at all.

- Request RSVPs and follow up on them.

You may make this as formal as you like by seeking paper RSVPs, or you can simply ask those who have been invited if they intend to attend so that you can have a rough headcount. No matter how you choose to go about accomplishing this, you need to find out who is planning to attend the event so that you can ensure that you have enough space and supplies to accommodate everyone. When you send out your request for RSVPs, be sure to add an inquiry as to whether or not the guest will be accompanied by a companion of some kind.

2. Difficult Questions That You Might Ask Yourself — You Shouldn't Worry About Them

Q: What takes place in your relationship if you like someone but you don't chat with them too often?

A: You should invite them to your party if you have adequate room for them to attend. They will most likely be quite appreciative of the invitation, and attending your party can provide you with a cause to speak to them more frequently. This may be the beginning of a friendship.

The Secret of a Meeting: Use Intimate Get-Togethers to Create Meaningful Connections

Q: The venue for my party is incredibly fantastic, but I can only invite one of my friends there. What should I do? It's a toss-up between these four candidates. What criteria should I use to choose who?

A: Pick a companion with whom you believe you would enjoy yourself to the fullest extent possible. Is there a specific person among your friends who makes you laugh more often than the others? There's a good chance that one of your buddies has already been to the extremely fantastic place that you're going. Pick the one individual that could make it the most successful gathering ever!

Q: What should you do if you know someone but don't know them very well but would like to invite them to your party so that you can get to know them better?

A: If you are familiar with someone but don't know them very well, you can invite them to your party.

The Secret of a Meeting: Use Intimate Get-Togethers to Create Meaningful Connections

That's an interesting proposition! One of the best ways to get to know someone is to invite them to a party you're hosting.

Q: I have a buddy who I would want to invite, but I don't because I know she will make trouble. What action should I take?

A: Before you finalize the party plans, you should have a conversation with her about the issue and establish some ground rules. If you know that she gets into the most disagreements with a particular individual, you should make every effort to avoid inviting that individual. Tell her that you won't be inviting her to your party because she is a gossip and a catty girl. If she is just one of those females that cause trouble all the time and don't stop, tell her that you won't be inviting her because of the way she acts. There is no point in inviting someone who will destroy your party, and if she won't be kind to you, then she is not a very good friend at all. There is no point in inviting someone who will spoil your party.

Q: What happens if you want to invite a friend but you know that they won't know anyone else who is going to be there?

A: Yes, getting to know new people is always a wonderful idea! If she is outgoing and self-assured, she will automatically mix with people; but, if she is somewhat reserved, you should enable her to socialize with the other friends that you have. It is hoped that once she is exposed to new environments and people, she will emerge from her cocoon.

3. The party's preparations, as outlined on the 10-point checklist

No matter if you're planning to host guests for the holidays or a forthcoming birthday, arranging a party can seem like a very difficult task. What details should be mentioned in the invitation? What types of food and beverages do you offer? Do you need to hire caterers for the occasion?

You shouldn't feel overwhelmed by all of these important questions, even though you should be asking yourself each one. You may streamline the duties that should be finished a month in advance rather than a few weeks beforehand and those that can wait until the days just before your event with the help of a simple party planning checklist.

1. Decide what type of party you want to throw.

The type of party you throw will affect how the event is organized. You're organizing a formal dinner; do you need to hire caterers? an unrestricted open house where visitors can come and go whenever they please? A leisurely barbecue in the backyard with outdoor games? Expert in entertaining and founder of Table + Teaspoon, the first business to provide a rent-the-table service, Liz Curtis says, "The kinds of parties you can throw in your home are only limited by your imagination." Pick the activity that appeals to you the most in terms of fun, and then stick with that format, is a solid rule of thumb to follow when choosing a party style.

2. Decide on a subject

The choice of a theme for your event is a personal one, but having one can help direct the selection of the event's décor and menu. According to Curtis, "Using a theme for your party can be as simple as selecting a color palette," and he says this. Make sure not to go overboard with a theme or general aesthetic for your home if you do so, since this may make your visitors feel cramped or give the impression that your home has been staged. When choosing your subject, Curtis suggests choosing "substance over kitsch."

3. Establish a budget for yourself.

The Secret of a Meeting: Use Intimate Get-Togethers to Create Meaningful Connections

The majority of the costs will likely need to be covered up front if you are hosting the party. Even if your home lacks the necessary tools, you may still need to decorate. What percentage of your budget are you willing to increase? whether the cost isn't too big, ask a few close friends whether they would be prepared to donate. They also want to partake in the pleasure, don't they?

One excellent strategy to save party costs is to ask guests to bring their own food. If everyone contributes, you won't have to pay for any of the food and you'll get to enjoy the festivities at the same time. You might even give particular people specific instructions, like having them bring drinks, ice, plates, napkins, and cutlery.

4. Get in touch with the suppliers

As long as you have the financial resources to do so, hiring experts is a great way to lighten the load. Designer and entertainment guru Sarah Spiegel advises, "Depending on where you live, it's a good idea to do this as far in advance as possible when you're planning catering."

If you have chosen to use outside services like bartenders, musicians, or caterers, be sure to have a thorough discussion about the specifics well before the event. Talk to them in advance about the music that will be performed, the food that will be served, and the timetable for the day. To guarantee a seamless party day, Kristine Cooke, an event planner and designer at Simply Charming Socials, advises giving detailed loading and parking instructions. Give explicit directions for parking and loading as well.

5. Establish a meal plan.

If you're going to prepare the entire meal at home, it's crucial to do as much as you can in advance. Cooke advises making a shopping list, selecting and reading recipes, and timing your purchases to avoid overloading your stove and oven. "Having a schedule for cooking is

The Secret of a Meeting: Use Intimate Get-Togethers to Create Meaningful Connections

always helpful because it ensures that courses and dishes will be ready at the appropriate time."

Food

Everyone looks forward to the supper the most because it is the main event of the evening. Identify the food that will go well with the time of day and the concept of the event, in addition to how the meal will be served, such as plated, cocktail style, grazing station, or self-serve, advises Cooke. "When planning the menu, consider not only how the food will be served but also what cuisine complements the occasion's theme and time of day." For instance, you generally wouldn't want to serve something like roasted duck, which is more appropriate for a formal dinner, if you were having a cocktail party.

Consider how nicely the meals on your menu complement one another as well. Spiegel says she always likes to offer something light and fresh to counteract any heavier items. Just my own preference, I guess. In the same vein, you want to make an effort to arrange your menu such that none of the products appear more than once. For instance, you shouldn't put pears in your side salad if you are making a dessert using pears.

Using the invitations as a guide, decide what to serve the guests after taking into account their dietary needs. However, some people could forget to respond, so it's a good idea to have at least one vegetarian option available that is also free of dairy and gluten, advises Spiegel. Maybe a salad or anything so you can hold the cheese in your hand comfortably."

Drinks

It is a good idea to consider the type of party you are having while choosing beverages. For an open house-style celebration, use a bar cart filled with pitcher drinks and portable food and drink options. At a formal dinner, wine, champagne, or sparkling water should be served before the course. Additionally, you want to have additional drinks on hand at the table in case any of the diners' glasses run dry during the course of the meal. Cooke suggests having both alcoholic and non-alcoholic beverages available.

6. Make Your Own Checklist

A lot of work goes into planning a party; to keep everything organized, create a thorough checklist of the necessary chores. Create a list of everything that has to occur a week prior to your celebration, and then assign dates to each item on the list, suggests Curtis. "This will keep you focused and organized." To avoid running about trying to get things done at the last minute, you should put everything on a to-do list, from the shopping items you need to the music you want to listen to. You won't have to rush to finish anything because of this.

7. Prepare the dishes and serving utensils.

The last thing you want on the day of your gathering is to discover that one of the dinnerware's plates or bowls is missing. Make sure all of your serving utensils are prepared at least two days before the party to avoid this awkward scenario. According to Spiegel, "I set it all out on a table, and you can even use a note to write what it is that you intend to serve in each dish." Make sure that everything, including your cutlery, is clean and polished before you set it all out.

8. Assemble a playlist

Every party needs music because it gives the event personality and keeps the crowd entertained during the night's inevitable lulls. A playlist should be created in advance, Spiegel suggests. It will greatly simplify your life. "I think it's a great method to pass the time to play music that suits your taste and style. Don't forget to consider what will make your guests happy as well.

9. Prepare the venue

The Secret of a Meeting: Use Intimate Get-Togethers to Create Meaningful Connections

Several days before to the arrival of your guests, make sure everything is in order. The advice Curtis gives, "If you forget anything, you'll have time to go shopping without interfering with your cooking schedule," is accurate. This comprises doing a thorough cleaning of all areas that are open to visitors as well as making any necessary preparations for any decorations. Don't forget the little details either, like providing fresh linens, colorful pillows, and extra seating to create a cozier atmosphere.

10. Add Some Ambience

You will be in charge of making the final adjustments on the day of your celebration. The simplest way to create a warm atmosphere, in Curtis' opinion, is to use lighting and floral arrangements. Go out and get some fresh flowers the day of your celebration, and then disperse them throughout your house, paying special attention to the rooms and areas where guests are most likely to congregate. Thanks to the combination of candles and flowers, your home will give off an air of grandeur just in time for the arrival of your loved ones.

Candles will aid in removing the need for harsh overhead lighting while also adding ambient lighting to your space. Dimmers or twinkling lights can also be used to generate this effect. Spiegel claims, "I prefer to use unscented candles because I don't want them to compete with the food."

Chapter 3: Let's Party!!

This is the story of John, who is one of my closest friends: "I have a severe phobia of nightclubs." I despise crowded, rowdy pubs. I am also prone to getting lost during concerts. Because of this, going out on Friday and Saturday nights as a person who is not 80 or older can be challenging.

He started inviting people to game evenings and dinner parties as soon as it was socially acceptable for them to be that age. Previously, they had been going to raves and bar crawls.

His first dinner party was a near-catastrophe in every sense of the word. There were a lot of snacks and sweets, but there wasn't enough actual food to go around. People arrived extremely late and departed rather promptly. His different circles of friends did not get along very well. And he was behaving erratically, running around like a madman.

The Secret of a Meeting: Use Intimate Get-Togethers to
Create Meaningful Connections

Notwithstanding everything, there was a glimmer of goodness. He recognized the potential in the evening, and several of his buddies inquired as to when he would repeat the experience.

BINGO! If even a single person is interested in what it is that you are doing, then you are onto something unique.

It was time to do a casual experiment with people. He planned to run for office in a variety of different parties, each of which would have different qualifications. Explore the possibilities, get a sense of the atmosphere, and discover how to host the ideal dinner party.

He uncovered some information that ran opposed to common sense as well as some seemingly trivial data that turned out to be crucial. I will relay all of that information to you.

1. What Most People Keep in Mind

Let's not put so much pressure on ourselves to arrange the ideal party, shall we? You certainly do not need to make the entire night consist of one bang and one bing after another for it to be enjoyable. People tend to recall three things in particular:

- The First Five Minutes: What goes down as people begin to arrive at the location? This is the item that people remember the most, much like their initial impression of an event.

- The High or the Low: Although it may seem strange, your event is required to have a high point. Otherwise? People only recall the terrible points, or even worse, they don't remember anything at all.

- The Previous Five Minutes: How people depart and the events that occur when they do so are other items that stay with them; this begs the question: why? The "RECENCY" effect is something that stays with us because we normally analyze the entire night immediately after we leave.

These are the three aspects of your event that require your attention first and foremost. If you are successful in doing so, your evening will be fantastic.

2. The Initial Impression of Your Event

This is what I look like immediately before I enter practically every event:

"What should I focus on doing first?"

"How do you think I look?"

"Do I know anyone?" is the question.

"Where should I hang up my jacket?"

When we first meet someone, how do you look, how do you sound, and how do you express yourself? I spend a lot of time talking about how to make a good first impression. Now I'd like to talk about the first impression that people get of your event. This is very important. In contrast to a personal brand, for which your first impression aim could be anything from impressive to forceful to amusing, I believe that every event should have the same two goals for its first impression:

The Secret of a Meeting: Use Intimate Get-Togethers to Create Meaningful Connections

Buzz equals coziness multiplied by excitement.

The majority of people, by the time they arrive at an event, are feeling at best overwhelmed, embarrassed, or anxious. At best, one should be enthusiastic, energized, and open-minded. Our goal is to get everyone into a positive state as soon as we possibly can. This is a surprising logistical consideration:

Make it incredibly simple for folks to enter the party you're throwing. Put up a notice indicating that the door is unlocked when you finish. Place directions on how to enter the property on the gate. Please forward any instructions via email. Keep in mind that individuals want to enter the building as quickly as they can. Make it simple for me.

Get off to a good start. The ideal scenario is to meet and greet individuals as soon as they enter the building. I make it a habit to position myself near the entrance so that I may extend a friendly greeting to anyone who enters. If not, you also have the option of having a distinct welcome section. Sometimes I'll hang a goofy piece of paper that reads, "Please remove your shoes and coats, and you are free to change into your pajamas whenever you like." Take a breath mint from the bowl down here, and make yourself at home!

Food and drink to soothe the soul. There is nothing that puts a person at ease more than having a drink in their hand and some food around. I always leave drinks where they can be quickly retrieved from the counter. I also make it a habit to provide folks with an enjoyable activity, to begin with. In the fall and winter months, my beverage of choice is warm apple cider, and in the spring and summer, I prefer blended cocktails of various kinds. It is a wonderful way to start things off, and it gets people interested. You have no idea how delighted people get whenever I ask them, "Would you like some spiced apple cider or hot cocoa?!"

I am a big supporter of chalkboard signs since they simplify everything.

I make use of them whenever customers walk in with
something amusing or a quip, and I also frequently place
them near the meal.

3. The Summit or the Valley?

The most common error made by hosts is the assumption
that guests will have fun participating in the same activity
throughout the entirety of the evening. Introverts and
ambiverts, in particular, find prolonged social interaction
to be excruciatingly painful.

The prospect of having to mingle for three hours at a party
can be overwhelming for most individuals, regardless of
how delicious the food is or how interesting the guests
are.

It is better when you can break the party up into what I
call highlights. You want to insert these into the typical
breakdown of a night. Here is how that looks:

The Secret of a Meeting: Use Intimate Get-Togethers to Create Meaningful Connections

First 30 min	Arrivals Appetizers Introductions	
Next 1 Hour	Main meal Main entertainment Deep conversation	Some people leave
Last 30 min	Dessert Intimate groups form	Most people leave

From this table, we can conclude that the ideal length for a gathering is 2 hours. It is:

Not too short: permit people to meet and get to know each other

Not too long: Leave this feeling of incomplete that will give people the wish to meet again

You want people to be aware of these periods so that you can schedule some programming that they can look forward to and that will also serve to break up the mingling. People tend to recall either the worst or the best part of an experience. All of these should be geared toward producing "Peak Moments." This is typically the most difficult time of the day if you do not have something planned for it.

Typical instances of the worst:

- Not being aware of who to speak to.

- Having a conversation with someone you hardly know that turns out to be awkward.

- Glancing at your watch and pondering the appropriate time to make your exit from the room.

- Not being able to find a place to sit or eat.

- Not having enough food or water to sustain oneself.

You should put your attention on important junctures. When you teach something to other people, when people laugh at something you said, or when you deliver a surprise of any type, those are the peak moments.

These are the options I like to go with:

The Secret of a Meeting: Use Intimate Get-Togethers to Create Meaningful Connections

- Unveiling a unique sweet or other food item – surprise s'mores! Fondue! The cake that's on fire!

- Revealing a customized cocktail or one based on performance – Buttery nipple shots! Margaritas that are on fire! Macaroons soaked in whiskey - yum!

- One of our go-to games is now in progress.

- There is a new game that we are playing.

We are going to try something brand fresh and exciting.

We are going to have some fun by watching a video.

The next thing on the agenda is a humorous toast!

Trying out a different way to kick off a conversation.

These are typically characterized by their little size. It is essentially the time when the entire group concentrates their attention on one game or announcement for a little period, which in turn prompts some of the members to smile, laugh, or ooh and aah. This is quite simple to do at less significant events. To facilitate smaller peak moments during larger gatherings, I have been known to place bowls of discussion starters strategically about the room.

4. The Influence of "RECENCY"

The tendency to remember the most recent item in a series is a phenomenon that can be seen in psychological research. When we leave an event, we frequently reflect on the previous evening as we either drive home or have a conversation with our partner on the way out the door. Therefore, if the final thing we saw or did was fantastic, it elevates the quality of the entire evening.

Because of this, wedding favors and party favors have proven to be very successful. EXCEPT FOR when they are distributed at the start of the game. The "RECENCY" effect is essentially nullified at weddings where the guests' party goodies are placed on each chair. This is a horrible practice. You would be better off placing them in a basket for folks to take with them as they leave.

The Secret of a Meeting: Use Intimate Get-Togethers to Create Meaningful Connections

My research has shown that the most popular periods for people to depart are as follows:

After the first hour, this section is reserved for persons who prefer to be alone, those who have another engagement, or those who are having a poor experience. It's all good! Get yourself ready for this. It takes place frequently.

After the final course has been served, if you are serving supper or dessert. Whatever time it is, there will always be some individuals who leave after dessert. Get yourself ready for this.

On the hour - People frequently establish agreements with themselves or their spouses; we will leave at ten o'clock tonight! We will be on our way at precisely 6 o'clock!

How can you make the most of these last seconds? After conducting a great deal of research on this topic, I have formed strong ideas. Let me know if you feel the same way in the comments below.

Avoid encouraging people to leave one by one.

The Secret of a Meeting: Use Intimate Get-Togethers to Create Meaningful Connections

I want everyone to have the impression that they are free to go whenever they see fit. The very WORST thing you could do is put someone under pressure to remain. This might frequently become the lowest point in their life. To ensure that everyone is aware of what is going to happen later in the evening, I will frequently let them know what they can expect by saying something along the lines of "We will do dinner and then dessert and then take it easy."

Alteration in Phase

Inform those present if you are going to be holding a game, dishing out food, or having a surprise. People are better able to understand that the night consists of stages and that they can escape at a phase change because of this.

Authorization to Leave

After each stage, I will typically announce something along the lines of "Hey, everyone! We are going to play a game next! You are under no obligation to participate, but I did want to give you a heads-up! This provides folks an easy way out, and it helps me to say my goodbyes nicely. " Or "Let's play one more game before we have dessert."

Even while I enjoy giving out modest parting gifts, I think that this is a bit excessive for a casual party. When I have a lot of food left over, I will sometimes hastily bag up some dessert and distribute ziplock bags with the words "Here are some munchies for the road!" to the guests who are departing."

5. The Paragon of Hospitality

If you want to be a great host, here is the one thing you should make sure to say throughout the entire evening:

"Hey! Have you ever talked to ___? It would be my pleasure to put you in touch!"

The second most interesting thing that has been said all night is:

"Would you like me to grab you some more food or drink?"

As a host, the best thing you can do for your guests is to provide them with exciting moments and connect with as many individuals as you can. It is not your responsibility

The Secret of a Meeting: Use Intimate Get-Togethers to Create Meaningful Connections

to ensure that everyone is having a nice time. The most helpful thing you can do is to provide them with both solace and excitement.

To host a fantastic party, you don't need to have the ideal party house, but you should spend some time making sure that the space you do have is optimized. First, simplify the process through which individuals can find things:

This is the restroom. Put up signage, make it as clear as possible, and make sure there is toilet paper and soap there. To a far greater extent than you may realize.

The location moves around. When I encourage people to switch locations, I find that they stay longer and have a better time overall. This might sound strange, but it has been my experience. Quite frequently, I will set up the appetizers at a location that is distinct from both the dinner and the dessert locations. Then, people move in distinct patterns and hover differently. We also have a porch, and we like to make use of it as a stop along the way when we have parties.

Food. Food allergies are extremely common in today's society. Gluten-free people should not have to guess what is safe to eat and what is not. Explain to vegans what they can eat and what they should avoid. This is merely an optional step that might be taken to show consideration for such guests. I try my best to make everybody feel like they are part of the family!

6. Think in Groups

It has come to my attention that EVERYONE enjoys events more when they contain a 'collective think' moment. I believe it is because it offers an opportunity for bonding, although I cannot confirm this. Permit me to elaborate. A "group think moment" is what I refer to as occurring when the entirety of the group participates in an activity together or when everyone experiences a moment of satisfaction at the same time. If at all possible, I make an effort to always have a group think moment as a potential peak time. How to do it:

The Secret of a Meeting: Use Intimate Get-Togethers to
Create Meaningful Connections

Give a toast, or encourage people to give a humorous toast.

- Get your game on.

Game nights, whether they are played formally or informally, are some of my favorites. There is a complete piece over here that explains how to host a gaming night. Even at large house parties, games can be played simultaneously by guests. For instance, there are occasions when I will give a toast at a large party in which I will thank everyone in attendance and then I will challenge the attendees to find the one person at the party who has either recently gotten a new tattoo, recently relocated from Ireland, or has a false accent. This typically causes a commotion in the community.

- The role of food in social interaction

There is a particular reason why I truly enjoy offering s'mores and fondue at the gatherings that I host. Everyone is encouraged to congregate in the same area and participate in the same activity at the same time.

Make use of various props.

I have a couch guest book that was given to me by my friends Stephen and Christine, and I frequently ask everyone to sign it before they go and read from it. My friends Stephen and Christine are wonderful people. Wine charms that people can speak about and food that people can utilize as conversation starters are two of my other favorite things.

7. Never Again Will You Forget Names

Have you ever found yourself in a scenario where you met someone at the beginning of a party, but when you run into them later on, after you've had a couple of drinks, or a few weeks later while you're out, you have no idea what their name is? It's a very awkward situation. Having to deal with something like that ever again is something I don't wish for you, so I'm going to show you how to recall names more quickly.

The Secret of a Meeting: Use Intimate Get-Togethers to Create Meaningful Connections

The challenge with names is that you have to actively engage your head to figure them out. When information is processed aurally, vocally, and visually, different regions of the brain become active. Engaging all of those components is necessary if you want to increase the likelihood that you will recall people's names. How to do it:

Auditory: Pay them your undivided attention when they speak their name so that you may concentrate on hearing it without having your mind wander to other things as you do so.

Verbal: Repeat their name after they have said it to you after they have finished saying it. Take, for instance, the greeting "Nice to meet you, Michael. So, Michael, what brings you to this place? Michael, what are you doing right now?"

Imagine all of the other people you know who share the same name, and then imagine this new person in a setting alongside all of those other people.

Consider how the name is spoken if you're having trouble remembering it. This is the most effective strategy you can use. You can activate areas of your brain that help you recall someone or something by associating their name with something that you already remember. For instance, I spoke with a person whose name was Siara. Because I've never encountered anyone else with that name before, I was unable to connect the person in question to anyone else. Instead, the sound of their name made me think of the Syrah grape kind, and they mentioned that they like drinking wine. Therefore, every time I see Siara, the wine, and its name immediately come to mind.

8. The Science and Art of the Ideal Handshake

It's important to shake people's hands at parties just as much as it is at job interviews. It is essential to be aware that different types of handshakes each have their unique characteristics.

People rarely think about the angle at which they are shaking hands, even though the majority of advice focuses on the hardness of your handshake and hiding anxiety indicators such as unsteady hands and sweaty palms. Have you ever extended your hand to someone, only to have them push it back in your face? This is a pretty authoritative stance to take. individuals who have alpha personalities often tend to give individuals a high-five handshake when they are trying to demonstrate their power. Whether or not they are aware of it, their brain has the innate knowledge that when they shake hands with someone and place their hand on top of the other person's hand, it makes the other person feel as though they have less authority. One variation of a domineering handshake occurs when one person pulls so strongly on the other person's hand that they are compelled to go in closer to the other person and begin to somewhat lose their equilibrium.

You should go for a nice, equal handshake rather than engaging in one of the dominant displays or letting someone perform one of them for you. This way, neither you nor the person you are speaking to will have the upper hand in the interaction. Getting this done is uncomplicated:

The Secret of a Meeting: Use Intimate Get-Togethers to Create Meaningful Connections

Keep your hand completely upright as you shake from top to bottom.

In the culture of the United States, one pump denotes the sentiment "It's good to see you," whereas two to three pumps express the sentiment "I'm so happy you're here."

Put the palm of your other hand on top of the palm of the other person's hand when you shake hands to give it a more personal feel. This results in the production of twice as much of the bonding hormone oxytocin, which is triggered when physical contact is made.

Caution is advised when employing this two-handed shake functionality. Some individuals find it awkward to be touched by somebody they do not know very well and will have a negative reaction to the increased level of closeness present in the situation. Reserving the double handshake for those who embrace, place their hands on the arms and backs of other individuals, and/or engage in other behaviors that indicate they are comfortable being touched is appropriate.

You can demonstrate your level of comfort with touch through body language, in addition to keeping an eye out for other people's attitudes toward physical contact. How to do it:

Open up your body and put your arms out if you wish to give or receive a hug.

If you don't want to hug someone, approach them at an angle such that when you shake hands with them, one side of your body is facing them and the other is facing away from them. This will prevent you from hugging someone.

The ideal way to greet someone when you don't want to shake their hand is to extend out your hand in a wave and say something to the effect of "Hi, it's good to see you."

Because it sets a favorable tone for the rest of your interactions at a party, mastering the art of the handshake is essential for having a good time at social gatherings.

9. Game-Changing Icebreakers

The Secret of a Meeting: Use Intimate Get-Togethers to Create Meaningful Connections

When meeting new individuals, many people have a natural tendency to feel shy. When around people they know well, a shy person's tendency toward reserve is less of an issue. Anxiety is brought on by novel experiences and encounters with unfamiliar people. If you are experiencing significant anxiety, new experiences, such as going off to college or even to a party where everyone will be new, may not seem as tempting as they otherwise would. Unfortunately, people tend to make the majority of their new acquaintances during parties, particularly in their early years after college and during college. If you want to make new acquaintances, the first challenge you'll need to overcome is getting to know the person you want to be friends with. abilities for getting to know you are the foundation for developing abilities on how to communicate in a relationship.

The following is a collection of useful strategies that will assist you in getting past the initial anxiety-inducing difficulties associated with meeting new people. Any gathering or social setting can benefit from the use of these seven tried-and-true methods for breaking the ice and getting to know one another.

These pointers are meant to be used in situations in which you are constantly surrounded by new people. At the same time, they are equally effective in scenarios in which there is only one potential contact nearby who you are interested in getting to know.

1. Make the decision that you are going to be the one doing the shopping, not the shopping.

You are scouring the area in search of interesting people for you to get to know better.

Think of social connection as a treasure hunt in which you are looking to learn intriguing things and possibly discover interesting people. Your goal is to connect with others who share your interests. Because you are the one who is searching, you are in a position of authority, which will help to alleviate any concerns that you might have.

2. Select a neighboring individual to talk to and make a connection with them. Remark something in the surrounding area to get the conversation started.

"Mm, these mini hot dogs have a delicious flavor; have you tried any of them yet?"

3. Please tell us about yourself.

When you exchange names with someone, you go from being two strangers to two people who are familiar with one another.

"Hello, my name is Cathy/Karl." (Shaking hands will get them to introduce themselves.)

If you're lucky, the name will provide a springboard for more conversation once you've introduced yourself.

"Oh, Grace. That's an intriguing name. People these days don't typically get named after qualities. How did that happen in your family?" "Oh, Grace. That's an amazing name.

4. Inquire with open-ended questions.

inquiries that invite significant information to be provided as a response, as opposed to simple yes/no replies, are referred to as open-ended inquiries.

The initial word is quite important. Questions that invite open-ended responses typically start with "what" or "how," as shown in the previous example. There are occasions when who, when, or where are also useful. Expressions such as "Are you," "Do you," "Have you," and "Did you"... are acceptable regularly. Simply put, they tend to elicit fewer pieces of information.

"How did it come to pass that your parents chose the name Grace for you? It appears to be a name with a history, which adds to its allure.

"Where in the world are you from?"

"What exactly do you do for a living?"

If you answer the question about yourself first and then ask the other person a question, the other person will likely experience less anxiety as a result of the interaction.

The Secret of a Meeting: Use Intimate Get-Togethers to Create Meaningful Connections

For instance, you may say, "I enjoy blues folk music like this. Not only do I enjoy listening to it, but I also enjoy having it playing in the background while I work. What genres of music do you like?"

5. Provide feedback on the response you have received.

Clarifying that you heard their response and are taking their opinions seriously by responding to it shows that you understood what they said.

A positive tone can be set by beginning with affirmative statements such as "I agree,..." or "I like...."

"I concur that the volume on this music is excessively loud at this point. "I wonder what would be an appropriate manner to turn the volume down." Before you ask your next open-ended question, talk together back and forth multiple times on that topic. If you don't, you may come across as a prosecuting attorney.

6. Provide information about yourself that is comparable to what has been discussed so that the conversation does not become overly lopsided.

Do you have something comparable to share about yourself?

"You may know me from Denver. Because of my desire to be near the mountains, I moved there a few years ago. I adore going on hikes."

7. Permit yourself to immerse yourself in the world of that other person.

Getting to know someone is similar to reading a book or watching a movie; you should try to take pleasure in the things you learn as the conversation progresses.

Enjoy yourselves!

Remember that you are the predator, not the prey; move on to the next individual if you find that you are losing interest.

10. After the celebration

I am grateful to you.

Be sure to express gratitude to the event's hosts, those who assisted you, and the attendees, and if you want to send thank-you notes, order them at the same moment as your invitations to save money on shipping.

Cleanup

Make sure that all of the equipment and decorations are taken down, and that the venue is left in the same condition that it was in when you found it, whether you hire a crew or you and your team of assistants do it.

Be Sure to Check Your Camera.

If you took any photos or films during the celebration, go through them and send them to your guests. Everyone will be grateful for such a thoughtful gesture, as the photos and videos will serve as the ideal memory that they will treasure for the rest of their lives.

The Secret of a Meeting: Use Intimate Get-Togethers to Create Meaningful Connections

Conclusion

We reach the destination as a meeting that lasts for two hours, which is just the right amount of time (not too short, not too long). There are three very important things that I want you to keep in mind:

Commit Yourself to a Particular Objective

Your get-together will be less generic and one-size-fits-all if you have a specific goal in mind from the very beginning of the planning process. Ask yourself these two questions before you even begin to plan an event: "Why are we gathering?" and "Who are we gathering for?" ...and "Why is it so important?" Ask "why" once more whenever you discover a new, more compelling justification.

Consider the Space in a Strategic Way.

It is stated that 90 percent of what makes a gathering effective is put in place before the event, and the location is the first thing that needs to be considered in this regard. Although it may be tempting to select a venue with a large capacity for your event, according to Parker, "bigger is not better." People who wander across a large room miss out on one of the most enjoyable aspects of a party, which is the possibility of running into someone new and striking up a discussion with them. If you are going to be hosting a large party, you should designate separate spaces for individuals to congregate.

Share a Tale Along with the Invitation

It is also tempting to consider sending a brief invitation that only includes the essential information. However, invitations provide the ideal chance to make your event feel more personal before anyone even enters the room.

The Initial Couple of Minutes Establish the Mood

According to several studies, the beginning and the finish of an experience are the parts that people remember the most. Despite this, we frequently give the least amount of thought to how we launch and wrap up an event.

If you are going to be the host, be sure to set some ground rules.

You are the cohesive force that keeps everyone else in place. "No one wants to be in a place where there is no law," said the man. "Do not abandon your visitors to their own devices. They are under your care, and it is your responsibility to keep them safe and connected.

Put an authoritative cap on your event.

We've all been there: it's getting late, guests are eerily sneaking their way toward the exit, and the party is slowly coming to an end. After that, add a touch of warmth by saying your goodbyes to each visitor as you walk them out the door. Give them a sweet treat or memento to take with them when they leave to keep the cozy feeling going for longer.